Author Biographies

Maurice Sendak

Charlotte Guillain

Heinemann Library
Chicago, Illinois

www.capstonepub.com
Visit our website to find out more information about Heinemann-Raintree books.

To order:
☎ Phone 888-454-2279
💻 Visit www.capstonepub.com
to browse our catalog and order online.

Edited by Rebecca Rissman, Daniel Nunn, and Sian Smith
Designed by Joanna Hinton-Malivoire
Picture research by Tracy Cummins
Production by Victoria Fitzgerald
Originated by Capstone Global Library Ltd
Printed and bound in the United States of America, North Mankato, MN

15 14 13 12
10 9 8 7 6 5 4 3 2

Library of Congress Cataloging-in-Publication Data
Guillain, Charlotte.
Maurice Sendak / Charlotte Guillain.
p.cm.—(Author biographies)
Includes bibliographical references and index.
ISBN 978-1-4329-5961-6 (hardback)
ISBN 978-1-4329-5967-8 (paperback)
1. Sendak, Maurice—Juvenile literature. 2. Authors, American—20th century—Biography—Juvenile literature. 3. Children's stories—Authorship—Juvenile literature. 4. Illustrators—United States—Biography—Juvenile literature. I. Title.
  PS3569.E6Z688 2012
  813'.54—dc22   2011016066
  [B]

042012
006656RP

Acknowledgments
We would like to thank the following for permission to reproduce photographs: Alamy Images pp. 17, 23b (© Illustration Works); AP Photo pp. 10, 23c (Susan Ragan), 20 (Mike Appleton); Corbis p. 11 (© Leon/Retna Ltd); Flickr p. 8 (© Jim Lambert); Getty Images pp. 4 (David Corio/Michael Ochs Archive), 5 (Spencer Platt/Getty Images), 9 (Robert Rosamilio/NY Daily News Archive), 12 (Jason Kempin), 16 (Jupiterimages), 18 (Todd Plitt/Contour), 19, 23f (Carol Guzy/The Washington Post); The Kobal Collection pp. 7 (RKO), 15, 21 (WARNER BROS); Library of Congress Prints and Photographs Division p. 6; Rex USA p. 13 (PETER BROOKER); Shutterstock pp. 14 (© Mr. Arakelian), 23a (© discpicture), 23d (© shupian), 23e (© Falconia).

Cover photograph of Maurice Sendak standing by a life-size scene from Where the Wild Things Are in 2002 reproduced with permission of Getty Images (James Keyser/Time Life Pictures). Back cover images of a Washington Ballet performance of 'Where the Wild Things Are' in 2007 reproduced with permission of Getty Images (Carol Guzy/The Washington Post).

Every effort has been made to contact copyright holders of material reproduced in this book. Any omissions will be rectified in subsequent printings if notice is given to the publisher.

Contents

Some words are shown in bold, **like this**. You can find them in the glossary on page 23.

Who Is Maurice Sendak?

Maurice Sendak is a writer.

He writes and draws the pictures for children's books.

Children all over the world love Maurice Sendak's books.

His most famous book is *Where The Wild Things Are*.

Where Did He Grow Up?

Maurice Sendak was born in 1928.

He grew up in New York City in the United States.

When he was a child, he was often sick and spent a lot of time reading.

He loved to watch cartoons and movies, such as *King Kong*.

What Did He Do Before He Was a Writer?

Maurice loved drawing when he was young.

He went to art school to study at night.

He also worked in a toy store, putting displays in the windows.

He worked and studied hard for four years.

How Did He Start Writing Books?

Maurice started drawing pictures for other people's books.

He started to become famous as an **illustrator**.

In 1963 he wrote and drew the pictures for *Where The Wild Things Are*.

This book made him famous all over the world.

What Books Has He Written?

After *Where The Wild Things Are*, Maurice wrote many other books.

Higglety Pigglety Pop is about a dog who goes looking for adventure.

In The Night Kitchen describes a boy's adventures in a strange dreamworld.

Outside Over There is about a girl who rescues her baby sister from goblins.

What Does He Write About?

Maurice's stories are often about dark and scary places and things.

His stories often happen at night when things are spooky and different.

Many of his stories are about brave children and other heroes.

They travel to other worlds and stand up to things that scare them.

How Does Maurice Sendak Draw His Pictures?

Some of Maurice Sendak's pictures are black and white.

Many **illustrators** draw pictures with pen and ink.

Maurice often uses a style called **cross-hatching**.

This is when lots of lines cross over each other.

What Else Does He Like to Do?

Maurice has a home in the countryside and an apartment in New York City.

He loves spending time with his dog, called Herman.

Maurice is also interested in the theater.

He has made costumes and **stage sets** for ballets and **operas**.

Why Is He Famous Today?

People all over the world buy Maurice Sendak's books.

He has won many **awards**, including the Caldecott Medal for *Where The Wild Things Are*.

A movie of *Where The Wild Things Are* was made in 2009.

People have also performed an **opera** of the story.

Timeline of Maurice Sendak's Life and Work

1928   Maurice Sendak was born in Brooklyn, New York.

1948   He started working in a toy store.

1963   *Where The Wild Things Are* was **published**.

1981   *Outside Over There* was published.

2009   A film of *Where The Wild Things Are* was made.

Glossary

award prize

cross-hatching style of drawing where lines cross each other closely

illustrator person who draws or paints pictures to go with a story

opera play that is set to music

published made into a book and printed

stage set scenery in the background on a theater stage

Find Out More

Books

Some of Maurice Sendak's books: *Where The Wild Things Are, Higglety Pigglety Pop, In The Night Kitchen,* and *Outside Over There.*

Braun, Eric. *Maurice Sendak (First Biographies).* Capstone, 2005.

Hurtig, Jennifer. *Maurice Sendak (My Favourite Writer)* Weigl Publishers, 2006.

Marcovitz, Hal. *Maurice Sendak (Who Wrote That?)* Chelsea House, 2006.

Websites

http://www.harpercollinschildrens.com/Kids/ AuthorsAndIllustrators/ContributorDetail. aspx?Cld=12708
Visit the Harper Collins website to learn more about Maurice Sendak and see inside some of his books.

Index